How to deal with Navigating Difficult Students

Strategies for Building Respect and Cooperation

John J Love

Copyright © John J Love 2023

All Rights Reserved

Table of contents

Introduction

Chapter One

The Challenges of Working with Difficult Student

Chapter Two

Setting Clear Expectations and Boundaries

Chapter Three

Using Positive Reinforcement to Encourage Good Behavior

Chapter Four

Teaching Problem-Solving Skills for Conflict Resolution

Chapter Five

Building Stronger Relationships with Your Students

Chapter Six

Using Restorative Justice Approaches to Repair Harm

Chapter Seven

Strategies for Dealing with Defiance and Disruptive Behavior

Chapter Eight

Supporting Students with Social, Emotional, and Behavioral Needs

Chapter Nine

Creating a Positive Classroom Culture for All Students

Chapter Conclusion

Empowering Students to Succeed

Introduction

Navigating Difficult Students: Strategies for Building Respect and Cooperation"

Are you tired of feeling frustrated and overwhelmed by students who challenge your authority and disrupt your classroom? Do you wish you had a roadmap for how to handle difficult behavior and build positive relationships with your students? Look no further! In "Navigating Difficult Students," you'll find practical, research-backed strategies for dealing with challenging behavior and fostering a supportive, respectful classroom culture.

From setting clear expectations and boundaries to using positive reinforcement and problem-solving techniques, this book offers a wealth of proven tools for managing disruptive behavior and building stronger connections with your students. Whether you're a seasoned educator or just starting, this book is a must-have resource for anyone looking to create a positive, engaging learning environment for all students.

"The Defiant Student: A Practical Guide to Managing Disruptive Behavior"

Are you struggling to manage a student who constantly defies your authority and disrupts your classroom? Do you feel like no matter what you try, you can't seem to get through to this student and improve their behavior? You're not alone. Working with defiant students can be one of the most challenging aspects of teaching, but it doesn't have to be.

In "The Defiant Student," you'll find a wealth of practical, research-backed strategies for managing disruptive behavior and building positive relationships with your most challenging students. From setting clear expectations and boundaries to using positive reinforcement and restorative justice techniques, this book offers a step-by-step guide for turning defiance into engagement and helping your students succeed. Whether you're a seasoned educator or just starting, this book is a must-have resource for anyone looking to create a positive, engaging learning environment for all students.

Chapter One

The Challenges of Working with Difficult Student

As an educator, you know that no two classrooms are the same. While some students may be eager to learn and well-behaved, others can be more challenging to work with. These students may defy authority, disrupt the class, or resist your efforts to teach them. Dealing with difficult students can be one of the most frustrating and stressful aspects of teaching, and it can be hard to know where to start.

In this chapter, we'll explore the common challenges of working with difficult students and the impact that these behaviors can have on your classroom. We'll also look at some of the root causes of difficult behavior, including social and emotional issues, learning difficulties, and environmental factors. By understanding the reasons behind difficult behavior, you can better tailor your approach and find strategies that work for your students.

Finally, we'll discuss the importance of building positive relationships with your students, no matter how difficult they may be. By establishing trust and respect, you can create a supportive, inclusive classroom where all students feel valued and motivated to learn. Whether you're a seasoned educator or just starting, this chapter will provide you with the foundation you need to navigate the challenges of working with difficult students and create a positive learning environment for all.

Chapter Two

Setting Clear Expectations and Boundaries

One of the keys to managing difficult students is to establish clear expectations and boundaries from the start. This helps to create a sense of structure and predictability in the classroom, which can be especially important for students who may struggle with impulse control or social skills. By setting clear expectations, you can help your students understand what is expected of them and encourage positive behavior.

In this chapter, we'll explore the importance of setting clear expectations and boundaries, and we'll discuss some strategies for doing so effectively. This may include creating a classroom contract or rules list, outlining expectations for behavior and work habits, and consistently enforcing consequences for inappropriate behavior.

It's also important to be explicit about the consequences of breaking rules or expectations and to follow through consistently when students do not meet these expectations. This helps students to understand the consequences of their actions and encourages them to make better choices.

In addition to setting expectations for behavior, it's also important to establish boundaries around personal space, physical contact, and other sensitive issues. By creating a safe and respectful classroom environment, you can foster a sense of trust and respect among your students and help them feel more comfortable and secure.

Chapter Three

Using Positive Reinforcement to Encourage Good Behavior

Positive reinforcement is a powerful tool for encouraging and reinforcing good behavior in students. When used effectively, it can help to build self-esteem, increase motivation, and improve relationships between teachers and students.

In this chapter, we'll explore the principles of positive reinforcement and discuss how to use it effectively in the classroom. This may include identifying specific behaviors to reinforce, choosing appropriate rewards, and using reinforcing language and gestures to show approval and appreciation.

It's important to keep in mind that not all rewards are created equal. The best rewards are those that are meaningful to the student and that support their goals and interests. It's also important to be consistent in reinforcing good behavior, as this helps students to understand that their efforts are valued and appreciated.

In addition to reinforcing good behavior, it's also important to recognize that there may be times when students need additional support or accommodations to meet expectations. By using positive reinforcement and making necessary accommodations, you can help students to feel more confident and motivated to succeed.

By using positive reinforcement to encourage good behavior, you can create a positive and supportive classroom environment where all students feel valued and motivated to learn.

Chapter Four

Teaching Problem-Solving Skills for Conflict Resolution

Conflict is a natural part of life, and students need to learn how to handle conflicts in a healthy, productive way. By teaching problem-solving skills, you can help your students to develop the tools they need to navigate conflicts and resolve issues on their own.

In this chapter, we'll explore the importance of teaching problem-solving skills and discuss some strategies for doing so effectively. This may include modeling problem-solving techniques, providing practice opportunities, and using role-playing and other interactive activities to help students apply these skills in real-world situations.

It's important to keep in mind that problem-solving skills take time and practice to develop. Therefore, it's important to be patient and to provide ongoing support and guidance as students learn to navigate conflicts and resolve issues.

In addition to teaching problem-solving skills, it's also important to model and encourages healthy communication and conflict-resolution strategies in the classroom. This may include teaching students how to express their needs and feelings in a respectful way, how to listen actively to others, and how to work together to find mutually satisfactory solutions. By teaching these skills, you can help your students to build stronger relationships and create a more positive and supportive classroom environment.

Chapter Five

Building Stronger Relationships with Your Students

Building strong, positive relationships with your students is an essential part of being an effective educator. When students feel connected to their teachers and classmates, they are more likely to be engaged in learning and motivated to succeed.

In this chapter, we'll explore the importance of building strong relationships with your students and discuss some strategies for doing so effectively. This may include getting to know your students as individuals, showing interest and care, and creating opportunities for positive interactions and connection.

It's important to keep in mind that building strong relationships takes time and effort. Therefore, it's important to be patient and to make an ongoing effort to connect with your students. This may include setting aside time to get to know your students, participating in extracurricular activities, and seeking out opportunities for positive interactions and connection.

In addition to building strong relationships with your students, it's also important to create a positive, supportive classroom culture. This may include establishing a safe and inclusive environment, promoting respect and kindness, and encouraging collaboration and teamwork. By building strong relationships and creating a positive classroom culture, you can create a sense of belonging and connection that will inspire and motivate your students to succeed.

Chapter Six

Using Restorative Justice Approaches to Repair Harm

When students engage in disruptive or inappropriate behavior, it's important to address the issue and address any harm that may have been caused. One approach that has gained increasing popularity in recent years is restorative justice, which focuses on repairing harm and rebuilding relationships rather than punishment.

In this chapter, we'll explore the principles of restorative justice and discuss how to use them effectively in the classroom. This may include using restorative circles or other structured processes to allow students to take responsibility for their actions, make amends, and learn from their mistakes.

It's important to keep in mind that restorative justice is not a one-size-fits-all approach, and it may not be appropriate for all situations. However, in many cases, it can be a powerful tool for helping students to take ownership of their actions and learn from their mistakes.

In addition to using restorative justice approaches, it's also important to recognize that some students may need additional support or accommodations to make amends and repair harm. By being understanding and supportive, you can help students to learn from their mistakes and move forward positively. By using restorative justice approaches, you can create a classroom culture that promotes healing and reconciliation, rather than punishment and isolation.

Chapter Seven

Strategies for Dealing with Defiance and Disruptive Behavior

Dealing with defiance and disruptive behavior can be one of the most challenging aspects of teaching. It's important to address these behaviors in a timely and consistent manner, while also recognizing that there may be underlying causes that contribute to the behavior. In this chapter, we'll explore a range of strategies for dealing with defiance and disruptive behavior, including setting clear expectations and boundaries, using positive reinforcement, and addressing the root causes of the behavior. We'll also discuss the importance of being consistent and fair in your approach, and we'll explore some strategies for de-escalating situations and maintaining a calm and professional demeanor.

It's important to keep in mind that what works for one student may not work for another, and it may take some trial and error to find the best approach for each student. It's also important to recognize that some students may need additional support or accommodations to succeed, and it may be necessary to work with other professionals (such as school counselors or behavioral specialists) to address more serious or persistent behavior issues.

By using a variety of strategies and being open to trying new approaches, you can help your students to overcome defiance and disruptive behavior and succeed in your classroom.

Chapter Eight

Supporting Students with Social, Emotional, and Behavioral Needs

Some students may struggle with social, emotional, or behavioral issues that can make it difficult for them to succeed in the classroom. These issues may include anxiety, depression, attention deficit disorder, or trauma. It's important to recognize that these issues can impact a student's ability to learn and to behave appropriately, and to provide support and accommodations as needed.

In this chapter, we'll explore strategies for supporting students with social, emotional, and behavioral needs. This may include providing a safe and supportive classroom environment, using positive reinforcement and other behavior management strategies, and working with other professionals (such as school counselors or behavioral specialists) to provide additional support.

It's important to keep in mind that every student is different, and what works for one student may not work for another. Therefore, it's important to be flexible and open to trying different approaches and to work closely with the student and their family to identify the best strategies for success.

By providing support and accommodations for students with social, emotional, and behavioral needs, you can help these students to overcome challenges and succeed in your classroom.

Chapter Nine

Creating a Positive Classroom Culture for All Students

Creating a positive classroom culture is essential for fostering a sense of belonging, respect, and engagement among your students. When students feel valued and supported, they are more likely to be motivated to learn and contribute to the classroom community.

In this chapter, we'll explore strategies for creating a positive classroom culture that is inclusive and supportive of all students. This may include establishing clear expectations and boundaries, using positive reinforcement to encourage good behavior, and promoting respect, kindness, and collaboration.

It's important to keep in mind that creating a positive classroom culture takes time and effort, and it requires the involvement and commitment of all members of the classroom community. By working together and supporting one another, you can create a positive, inclusive environment that promotes success for all students.

In addition to creating a positive classroom culture, it's also important to recognize that some students may face additional challenges or barriers to success. By being understanding and supportive, and by providing accommodations as needed, you can help these students to overcome obstacles and succeed in your classroom.

Chapter Conclusion

Empowering Students to Succeed

In this book, we've explored a range of strategies for dealing with difficult students and creating a positive, supportive classroom environment. While working with difficult students can be challenging, it can also be incredibly rewarding, as you have the opportunity to make a positive impact on the lives of your students and help them succeed.

In this final chapter, we'll summarize the key takeaways from the book and discuss some final thoughts on empowering students to succeed. This may include reinforcing the importance of building strong relationships, using positive reinforcement and restorative justice approaches, and providing support and accommodations as needed.

It's important to keep in mind that every student is different, and what works for one student may not work for another. Therefore, it's important to be flexible and open to trying different approaches and to work closely with your students and their families to identify the best strategies for success.

By using the strategies outlined in this book and being open to trying new approaches, you can empower your students to overcome challenges and succeed in your classroom and beyond.

www.ingramcontent.com/pod-product-compliance
Lightning Source LLC
Chambersburg PA
CBHW050327220526
45465CB00005B/2165